modern country mary norden

modern country mary norden

This book is dedicated to Ann, with love

First published in Great Britain in 2000 by

Conran Octopus Limited

A part of Octopus Publishing Group

2–4 Heron Quays

London E14 4JP

Commissioning Editor **Denny Hemming**

Project Editor **Jo Richardson**

Copy editors **Jo Richardson, Galiena Hitchman**

Art Editor **Georgina Rhodes**

Stylist **Mary Norden**

Production **Sue Sharpless**

British Library Cataloguing-in-Publication Data.

A catalogue record for this book is available from the British Library.

ISBN 1 84091 092 5

Printed in China

above

The striated effect of
a wooden fence
against dried grass
finds its counterpart in
a striped matress cover
(far right), faded over
the years to beautifully
muted shades of taupe
and dark grey. Sunset

and storm clouds
suggest an unusual
and dramatic pairing
of colours, while skeins
of light and dark rope
evoke a more classical
colour scheme.

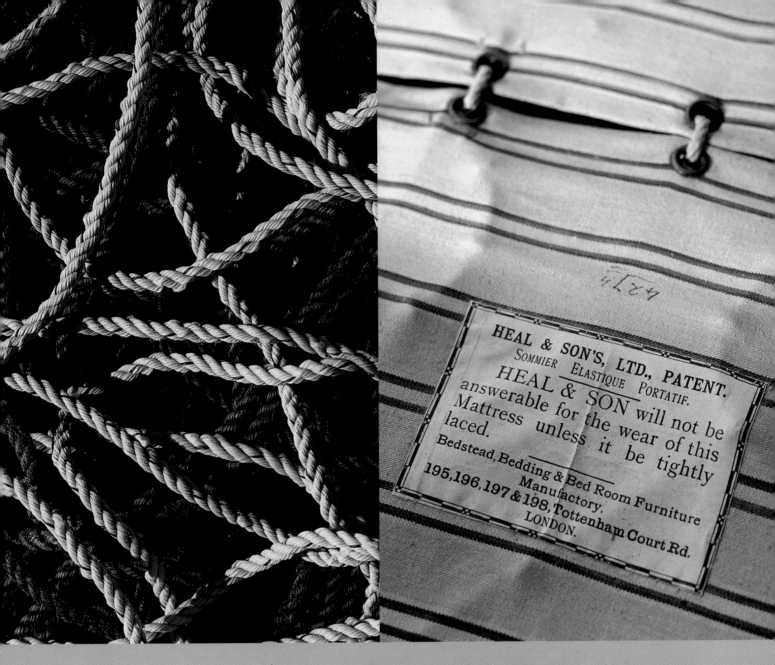

introduction

Just as fashion is reflecting a nostalgia for simpler, more innocent times, so natural materials and craftsmanship are becoming more important in our homes. This wistful rural mood is the very opposite of the hard-edged minimal style that recently defined a chic interior. Rustic household items such as butler sinks, lime-washed wooden trugs an tables, enamel pots and woven willow baskets are de rigueur, even in urban homes. The modern country home is minimally decorated. This does not mean creating interiors that are spartan and unfriendly, but rather rooms that are plainly furnished in a way that evokes timeless comfort and

informal style. Furniture is chosen for its simple shape and for function, as well as for craftsmanship and quality of materials. Similarly, fabrics, such as old linen sheets and woollen tweeds, are valued for their textures, as well as subtle colourings and patterns. Nature is an enormous inspiration in the modern country home, from the obvious natural rhythm of the seasons, that dictates woolly blankets, log fires and thick curtains in winter, sheer muslins and cool linens in summer, to more subtle influences. It is a never-ending source of colour combinations, pattern and texture, from the stripes of a snail's shell to the regular furrows of a ploughed field. The book's four chapters look at these topics in detail. Chapter one, Colour, shows how to interpret ideas from

above

A natural scene divided by bands of colour – pale water, dark stems of a stand of rushes topped with uniformly plumed flower heads, set against a dark woodland backdrop – gives an accurate impression of how similarly combined colours will look in the home. Here the look has been translated into white walls washed to dado height with a smoke-grey distemper, with darker accents provided by the painted woodwork.

Degrees of colour
in tree trunks on a
misty day can be
interpreted as a fabric
such as ticking, with
stripes of varying
thickness and tone.
Everyday wear and tear
can reveal unexpected
colour combinations,
when paint rubs away
to expose bare wood.

Frosted fennel leaves
are as fine as any
lace trimming. A bold
illustration of the
contrast between hard
and soft – feathery
silhouettes of sparrows
against the strong lines
of an iron railing.

the landscape into successful interior colour schemes. Chapter two, Texture, looks

at traditional materials such as wood and stone, as well as embellishing fabrics to

create textural interest. Pattern and Plain, chapter three, explores techniques for

mixing patterned fabrics and plain colours, and even pattern with pattern, combining

floral designs with stripes, checks or yet more florals. The final chapter, Atmosphere,

demonstrates the impact of natural light within the home.

Using this book as your guide, you can take inspiration from everything around you,

from a handful of pebbles, to the grandeur of a storm sweeping in from the sea. You

will be surprised at how much information there is all around, once you begin to look.

colour

Colour plays an essential role in creating style and atmosphere, whether used as an overall decorating scheme or to accent a monochromatic interior. To help with the process of selecting and using colour, follow nature's unerring example. Your immediate surroundings can provide an effective springboard for ideas – a stormy sky may suggest a sophisticated room dressed in slate grey and shades of blue while the varying tones of driftwood, pebbles and sand could inspire a harmonious interior of soft, bleached colours. Study, too, the contrasts of colour – red berries framed by the silver of a spider's web, bold black markings inside a red tulip or even something as simple and dramatic as the setting sun.

Just as a full-blown ruby red rose is shown to best effect in a simple glass vase with space and light around it, so an elaborately patterned bedspread of deep reds and purples is perfectly framed and contained by a simple, airy interior of pale cream walls and dark oak floor. Casually strewn pillows, covered with old linen tea-towels with a single crisp red stripe, also have a freshening effect and add to the mood of tranquillity.

colour in repose Red is a colour that wants to be noticed. Think of a field of summer

poppies, red apples or the berries of a holly tree; their bold hues clamour for attention.

Scarlet, crimson, magenta and cerise all bring life to a room because they are exciting,

dramatic colours. Even used on a small scale, red makes a striking feature. Other

moods or images can be created, depending not only on the shade of red but what it is

mixed with. For example, classic red and white gingham has a fresh feel, while the

purple-red of old-fashioned roses, as used here, can appear sombre unless combined

with off-white or cream. This spacious interior, although informal, looks smart with the

red and purple striped throw set against a wall the shade of cream lace or linen.

mellowed tones Nature's elements have their own unique way of tempering colour, modulating its harsher tones and giving it an attractive worn quality which conveys comfort. Mellow colours are easy to live with. Think of a new terracotta plant pot – bold and even in colour and texture – weathering to a characterful chalky pink, rich in tonal variation, that blends with its context. You can recreate this effect on interior walls by colourwashing over plaster, first sealed with off-white emulsion. Dilute water-based paint in your chosen colour with about half as much water to produce a semi-transparent glaze, and build up the colour in roughly applied layers, with a final layer of off-white glaze for a dusty, aged look. Terracotta pinks and yellows bring a soothing warmth to a living room or bedroom, evocative of hot summers past. Fabrics, too, are changed over time; exposure to sunlight knocking back original colours and patterns to worn, faded versions. When using old fabrics that have a country or traditional look, think laterally and use them out of context to soften hard-edged rooms. Striped canvases originally hung in doorways in the summer, make striking table runners, or can be hung individually, banner-style, behind a bed as a giant headboard.

*Slanting sunlight filters
through a child's old
tweed jacket, bringing
warmth and life to its
sombre, workaday
tones. In the same way,
the severe colours of
a utilitarian striped
canvas curtain have
been mellowed by the
sun's rays to create
a subtle-toned textile.
It now makes an ideal
table runner for an old
trestle table, teamed
with an attractively
care-worn office chair.*

quiet complementaries Colour is like music; it has an inherent ability to create mood. The soothing blue of catmint, the stimulating pink of a rose or the mellow tones of an autumnal orchard are all prime examples. But the moods these colours inspire will change according to the quality of light. No colour stays the same throughout the year, or even through the day. So when choosing colours, study them in context at different times of the day in both natural and artificial light. Think about how and when you want to use the room. An interior flooded with light can take a deep or louder shade of colour than one that is north-facing. For example, citrus yellows and cobalt blue can appear strident unless bathed in strong sunlight. Opt instead, as illustrated here, for the softer end of the yellow spectrum and complement it with a soft shade of blue. Another important factor to consider is how colours react with one another. Certain colours make perfect partners – blue and white china and fabrics always look wonderful against a yellow backdrop, just as the golden yellow of a field of wheat in summer is enhanced by the blue of a cloudless sky. Bright red and blue, if kept apart by plenty of white, also work well together, but can become too dense and heavy if placed side by side.

above

Even a bleak, wintry seascape can trigger new ideas for combining colours. Beach huts strung out along the shoreline form a row of cream blocks defined by the moody greys of gathering storm clouds behind. The glowering darkness blacks out their windows to create starkly contrasting rectangles. This graphic juxtaposition of light and dark is reflected in a patchwork quilt of indigo and cream.

colour components The natural landscape can help you to explore new, subtle ways of applying and composing with colour to create changes of mood from room to room. Stormy winter skyscapes, menacing and oppressive, reveal the whole spectrum of graduating tones of a single colour, from the darkest grey through to platinum. Brought inside, this colour scheme has quite a different effect, bringing a reflective, sophisticated feel to, say, a living room. Breezy morning spring skies offer quite a different palette – pastel blues washed with white or pearly grey, ideal for imparting a fresh airiness to a small bedroom or bathroom. By contrast, the intense blue of a cloudless sky is a bold, stimulating choice for a room that is often bathed in sunlight.

right

Group together traditional objects and materials in coordinating colours and varying tones. Use them as colour and texture palettes to gauge their combined effect. Here, a 1950s picnic box, bundles of hessian braid and a piece of tweed fabric provide a study in blue, grey and brown.

left

Inspired by the colours of northern winter skies, from platinum and cloud-grey to anthracite, this elegant striped curtain is made in shades of grey and blue linen. Despite the boldness of the pattern, the curtain is very simple to make – see the instructions for making a patchwork bedcover on page 29.

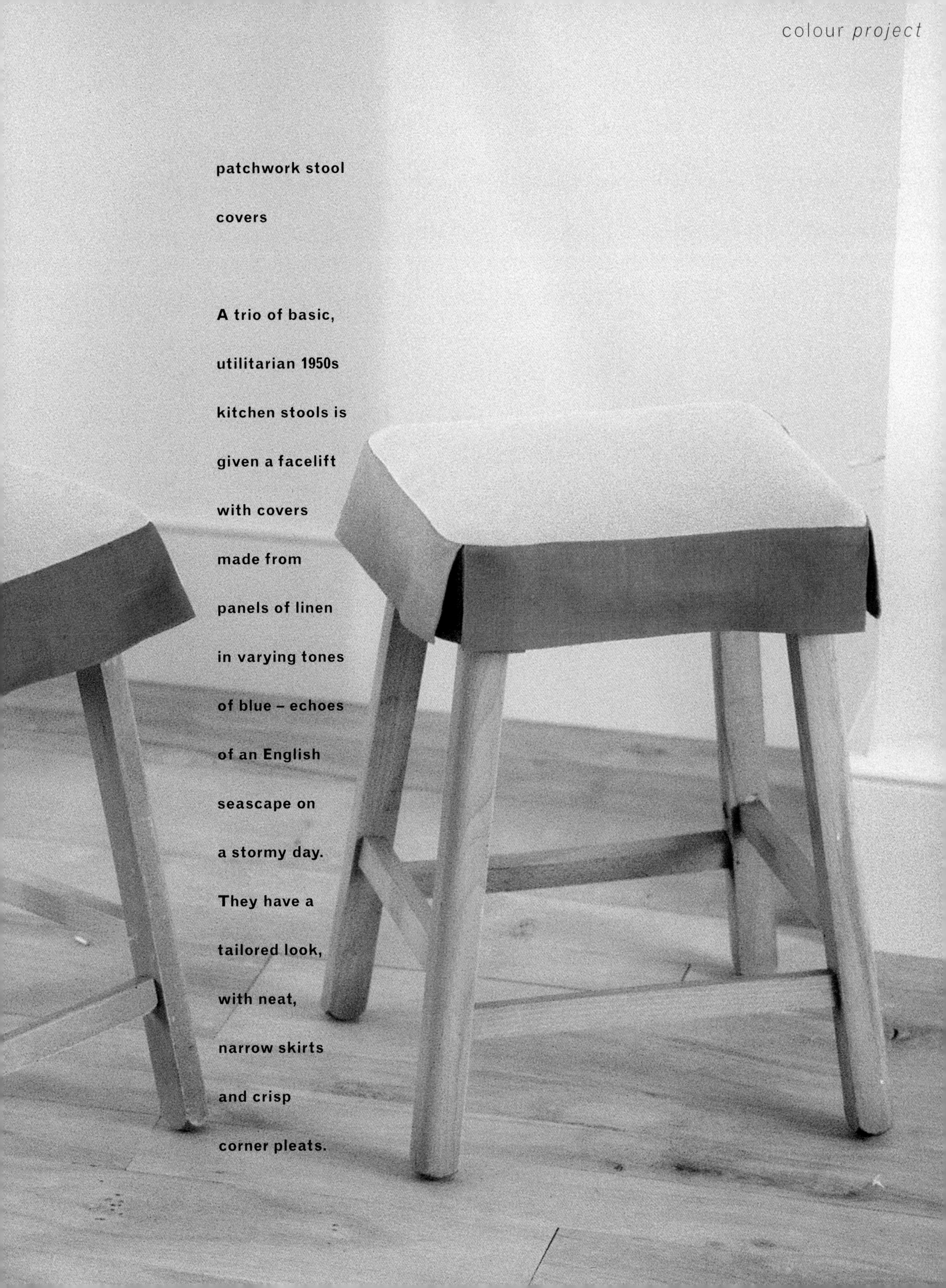

patchwork stool

covers

A trio of basic,

utilitarian 1950s

kitchen stools is

given a facelift

with covers

made from

panels of linen

in varying tones

of blue – echoes

of an English

seascape on

a stormy day.

They have a

tailored look,

with neat,

narrow skirts

and crisp

corner pleats.

materials

Each stool cover is made in three different shades of blue. Five pieces of fabric are used: the main piece covers the top and four pieces make up the stool skirt, with matching colour on opposite sides.

For each stool

■ *For the stool seat cover: plain linen fabric in a colour of your choice. (Approx 50cm [20in] x 90cm [36in] wide.)*
■ *For the stool skirt: plain linen fabric in two different shades of your main colour choice. (Each approx. 40cm [16in] x 90cm [36in].)*
■ *sewing thread*
■ *self-adhesive Velcro*

1 Measure the length and width of your stool seat, then mark the dimensions on to the main piece of fabric for the seat cover, adding a 1.25cm (½in) seam allowance on all sides. Cut out.

2 For the first two pieces of the skirt, begin by establishing the length of one edge of the stool seat. Add 12.5cm (5in) to this to allow for seams and corner pleats. Now establish the depth of your skirt (approx. 12cm [4½in]) and add a further 3.5cm (1½in) for seam allowance and hemming. Measure and cut out two fabric pieces to these dimensions (for opposite sides of the stool). Next, measure the length of the remaining sides of the stool and, again allowing for seams and hems, cut out pieces from the other shade of fabric, to the same depth as before.

3 With right sides together and alternating the different coloured fabric pieces, pin each skirt panel to the next along the short edges to form a continuous, two-tone loop. Machine stitch, taking a 1.25cm (½in) seam allowance, then press the seams open. For the hem, fold one long edge of the skirt 2.5cm (1in) to the wrong side then press. Hem in place and press again.

4 Mark vertical lines across the depth of the skirt 10cm (4in) on each side of each of the skirt panel seams. Fold along these marked lines so that the two folds meet exactly over each seam, to form a pleat. Pin and baste the pleats in position.

5 With right sides together and raw edges aligning, pin the skirt to the seat cover, positioning the pleats exactly at the corners. Machine stitch, taking the 1.25cm (½in) seam allowance. Press the finished cover thoroughly, attach two strips of Velcro to the seat top and inside the cover and place on the stool.

Colour notes

These covers would work equally well in other colour combinations, depending on the mood that you want to create. Try shades of white and cream for a calm, restrained scheme. Think of milk, old linen, snow and worn pebbles gathered from the beach; colours that are barely there. When using neutral tones, add texture, otherwise the effect can be bland, so use thick linen fabrics or even slubby raw silks.

For a richer, warmer feel, choose a mixture of earthy tones. Shades of terracotta, old leather, worn wooden furniture and natural pigments such as raw or burnt umber all offer suitable inspiration.

patchwork

bedcover

This contemporary take on the traditional craft of patchwork also works well for curtains. Large rectangles of plain linen fabric in soft, mellow shades of green, yellow and beige, evoking the familiar patchwork of fields in spring and early summer, are sewn together to create a simple yet striking bedcover.

materials

To make a cover to fit a 90cm (3ft) wide bed.

■ *9 rectangles of plain linen fabric, each measuring 66 x 86cm (26 x 34in), in an assortment of green, yellow and beige shades*
■ *4m (4½yd) of 145cm (54in) wide cotton sateen curtain lining*
■ *sewing thread*

1 On a flat surface, arrange the rectangles of fabric right side and portrait way up to form 3 rows of 3 patches each. When you are happy with the colour arrangement, with right sides together, pin the first row of patches together, joining them along the long edges. Machine stitch, taking a 1.5cm (⅝in) seam allowance. Repeat with the remaining 2 rows of patches to form 3 strips. Press the seams open.

2 With right sides together, pin the three strips of patches together, making sure that the seams joining the individual patches together in each strip are aligned. Taking in a 1.5cm (⅝in) seam allowance, machine stitch and press the seams open.

3 Cut the length of lining fabric into two equal pieces. Taking a 1.5cm (⅝in) seam, machine stitch the two widths of fabric together down the sides. Press the seam open. Mark the dimensions of the patchwork bedcover on to the lining fabric and cut out to fit.

4 With right sides together, pin the patchwork bedcover to the lining fabric. Taking a 1.5cm (⅝in) seam allowance, machine stitch around the edges, leaving a 50cm (20in) opening along one edge. Trim the corners to remove excess fabric. Turn the cover right side out. Turn in the raw edges of the opening and slip stitch to close. Press well.

above

Bundles of yarn dyed with weld (above, centre), the most commonly used natural dye, show the variety of vibrant yellows and greens that can be obtained from just one type of plant. From mustard through muted lime to mossy green, this range of tones captures the same subtle diversity of colour found in the natural landscape, as in this rolling carpet of young, green wheat. Natural dyes take best on wool or silk.

vegetable hues Colour can literally be taken from nature in the form of vegetable extracts used to dye fabrics in the age-old country tradition. Flowers, leaves, roots, bark, even vegetable skins can be used to create rich and refined shades of colour that are infinitely variable and therefore unique. The season in which the plant material is harvested has the greatest effect on the final colour, but the growing conditions, such as rainfall and soil type, also have an influence. An additional factor is the type of fixative used, usually a metallic salt, known as a mordant. The most common is alum (potassium aluminium sulphate), which is typically then combined with cream of tartar (tartaric acid). The colours neverthless fade but with an exquisite delicacy.

raw silk dyed

with nettles

Even weeds gathered

from your garden

can be put to

decorative use as

fabric dyes.

The humble nettle

produces a beautiful

soft, greenish-yellow

dye, as we can see

in this project. After

dyeing, the textured

raw silk fabric was

used to make a

simple, informal blind

at a small window,

loosely gathered up

with rustic string tied

in casual bows.

materials

The following quantities are for dyeing 1.5m
(1½yd) of 90cm (36in) wide raw silk fabric

■ *15–20 litre (3–4 gallon) enamel container*
■ *40g (1½oz) alum (potassium aluminium
sulphate), available from pharmacies*
■ *2 teaspoons cream of tartar (tartaric acid)
available from grocery stores*
■ *1 bucket of fresh nettle tops, about 9 litres
(2 gallons) in volume*
■ *large piece of muslin*

1 Wash, rinse and wring out the fabric.

2 Fill the enamel container with 9 litres
(2 gallons) of warm, soft water. Mix the alum
and cream of tartar with a little boiling water
and add to the water. Stir well to dissolve.
Heat the enamel container on a cooker top.
When the water is hand hot, immerse the wet
fabric in it and simmer for at least an hour,
stirring occasionally. Turn off the heat and let
the liquid cool before lifting out the fabric.

3 Pour away the liquid and rinse out the
container. Fill with 9 litres (2 gallons) of fresh
water. Put the nettles onto the muslin, gather
the corners together and knot. Lower into the
water with the fabric. Slowly bring the dye
bath to a simmer and continue simmering for
½ to ¾ hour. At intervals, remove the bag from
the bath and agitate the fabric in the liquid to
make sure that the dye is evenly dispersed.

4 Once the fabric is evenly dyed, remove from
the enamel container and rinse well until the
water runs clear. Hang up the fabric to dry.

5 Make up the dyed fabric as you wish, into
a blind as shown or cushion covers.

earthy notes The more subdued tones of the natural world are ideal for creating an understated contemporary look. Unlike the often lifeless monochromatic schemes of urban chic, those that truly reflect nature's depth and complexity are never dull. Even the most modest plants are full of textural colour. Patches of lichens on old stone walls reveal many shades of yellow and brown, while moss-covered banks are made up of separate tones of greys and greens that merge to give a muted green hue. Tweed fabrics and woven wool blankets both offer this rich tonal quality, blending colours beautifully. Use them for upholstery projects, slipcovers and throwing over beds or tables, and even for making into curtains.

above

A flavour of true country is brought to a surburban garden with a simple wooden table decked with a trio of table runners made from a Liberty lawn print. The tiny florals meld into a textured bed of grey-greens, which in turn blends into the natural surroundings. The tableware is earthy in both nature and colour – old wooden punnet buckets and roughly woven flax napkins of sandy loam hues, an earthenware bowl of red-brown clay and a slate-bottomed tray.

natural drama At times, nature appears to push the boundaries of colour theory to its limit, experimenting with the properties of colour and its relative proportions. Weather, though often passing fleetingly across the countryside, plays an enormous part in this drama of breaking the accepted rules. The dense grey of thunderous storm clouds gathering over a field of luminous yellow rapeseed in full bloom is dramatic not just because of the two contrasting colours but because of the scale and the relative proportions in which they appear. The same concepts can be translated into an interior. Before decorating a room, think about its basic structure and the arrangement of its architectural features. What is it that you wish to accentuate or even disguise, and what kind and scale of furniture is appropriate? In the room shown here, the walls have been horizontally divided into two contrasting bands of colour, making an exciting visual statement. The scale of the room, with its high ceiling, thick walls and lack of clutter, is emphasized by the use of colour. In addition, the painted walls provide a theatrical backdrop for the grand scale of the bed and the elegant high-backed chair. The overall effect is one of serene sophistication, applicable to any modern home.

right

*This interior, inspired
by the horizon on pages
38–9, employs a different
palette and assumes an
alternative personality
in this interior. The wide
band of creamy white,
extending seamlessly
into the ceiling, with a
narrower band of smoke
blue-grey below, creates
an atmosphere of
coolness and calm.
It has a gently refining
effect on the solidity of
the room. The cream
and yellow variation, by
contrast, injects drama
and radiant light into a
dull, dark stairway.*

Inspired by the interior on the opposite page, old galvanized flower buckets were painted in contrasting bands of cream and yellow ochre. Before painting, scrub each bucket thoroughly to remove any dirt, then allow to dry. Apply two coats of cream eggshell paint. When the paint is dry, wrap a length of masking tape around the bucket to mark the height of the yellow band. Apply one coat only of yellow ochre eggshell paint.

colour accenting Harmonious colour schemes, although easy to live with and beautiful to look at, sometimes need a little excitement. Consider the parallel in nature with the planting scheme of a country garden. Green, in its rich range of shades and textures, is the predominant colour. Against this unassuming and quiet background, flowers provide the impact. Placing a vase of flowers in a room is the easiest way of adding a splash of colour to an otherwise calmly composed scheme. Another way of dropping in accents of colour is through the use of soft furnishings – cushions, curtains, blinds and tablecloths. Besides introducing a change of pace, a colour element can also highlight an interesting architectural feature – a stairway, a door frame or a fireplace.

above

These two pictures illustrate the effect of adding or not adding an accent to a colour scheme. The painted turquoise barn blends well with the green of the countryside. If the sludgy brown roof or even the windows had been painted red, this would have created an exciting contrast, making the features of the barn more pronounced. The bright touches of aquamarine used in this kitchen add vitality to an otherwise simple, monochrome interior.

plaid padded

headboard cover

A tie-on padded

cover is an

inexpensive way

of creating a

comfortable

headboard,

and gives the

opportunity to

introduce a colour

accent. **C**hecked

shirt cotton was

used here, but other

traditional fabrics,

such as woollen

blankets, pieces of

patchwork and plain

linen sheets, would

also work well.

materials

■ *cotton fabric*
■ *matching sewing thread*
■ *medium-weight polyester wadding*

1 To calculate the fabric quantities required, measure from the mattress to the top of the headboard and multiply by 2. The width of the fabric required equals the width of the headboard. (If you are using patterned fabric, an allowance of extra fabric must be made for matching the pattern at the seams, particularly for checks and stripes.) Cut a top and bottom panel from the fabric to the calculated dimensions, adding a 1.5cm (⅝in) seam allowance all round.

2 Cut 12 strips of fabric, each measuring 4 x 40cm (1½ x 16in), and make the ties. Press in a 5mm (¼in) fold around the edges of each strip, then fold in half along the length. Pin, then machine stitch along the one long and two short open edges.

3 Place one of the fabric panels over the headboard so that it hangs down the front of the headboard to the top of the mattress. Using pins, mark the position of 3 evenly spaced pairs of ties on the left, right, back and front of the fabric. Lay the fabric panel on a flat surface, right side up. Pin one tie on each marker at right angles to the sides of the fabric panel, with one short edge just protruding beyond the fabric panel edge and the tie length laying across the panel towards the centre.

4 With right sides together, pin the top and bottom fabric panels together. (The ties will be on the inside.) Machine stitch down the two sides and along the bottom edge of the cover, taking a 1.5cm (⅝in) seam allowance. Leave the top edge open. Turn the cover right-side out and press.

5 Cut a piece of wadding slightly smaller than the finished cover and insert into the cover through the opening. Fold in the raw edges of the opening and slip stitch to close. Place the padded cover over the headboard and tie the ties in bows at the sides to hold it firmly in position.

Colour notes

Being a strong colour, purple can be difficult to use. Mixing purples together on a small scale can make an exciting colour scheme in an interior, but their vividness needs to be reined in by neutral colours (not white, which is too stark a contrast). In this case, the subtle cream of the old linen sheets, the biscuit brown of the checked hessian and the warm brown stripe that runs through the shirt fabric all help to dilute the impact of the purple. The fact that this bedroom is south-facing and enjoys plenty of natural light also helps to play off the strength of the colour.

To coordinate with the purple-checked headboard cover, a bedcover has been made from wool tweed. As with many tweeds, this fabric gives the impression of being one, uniform shade of deep purple, but on closer inspection it reveals a glorious mix of different colours – bright violet, blue and rich brown. This is the way colour so often works in nature – depicted here in the irises displayed in a bucket vase at the bedside.

texture

Life would be extremely boring without texture. With only solid slabs of colour to look at, there is no interesting detail to hold the attention, however briefly. But there is no shortage of texture for the modern country home, indoors and out. Materials left out of doors rapidly acquire texture as they weather and age. Metal becomes pitted and roughened by rust, wood splits and twists, paint flakes and bubbles. You can bring texture indoors simply by carrying in a basket of logs or a piece of driftwood to put on the windowsill, or you can translate what you see into your own ideas. Experiment with lighting to create interesting shadows on rough surfaces, and accentuate texture by grouping single-coloured objects, with rough alongside shiny or smooth.

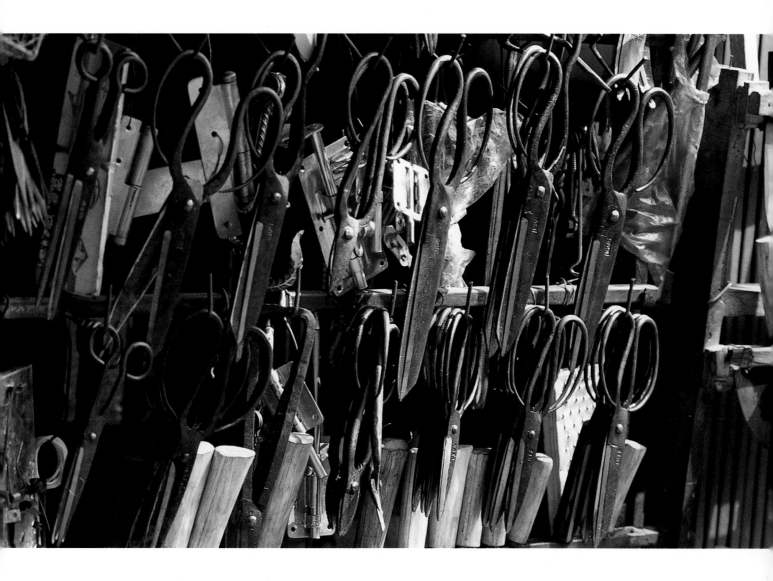

warm and cold Materials like wood and stone are intrinsically solid yet are very

different to touch. The versatility of wood allows many different finishes and uses, but

whether French polished or roughly planed, it is always warm and inviting. Stone, by

contrast, is cold and unforgiving. Although texturally pleasing, stone underfoot can be

extremely cold without a scattering of rugs. Try using it instead for less obvious

applications: an old stone trough for a sink or a stone bench in the hall.

Steel is a traditional material increasingly popular in the home. With a patina of age it

looks well with natural wood (see above). Translate this partnership for the modern

country home by mixing steel chairs with a wooden table (as on the following page).

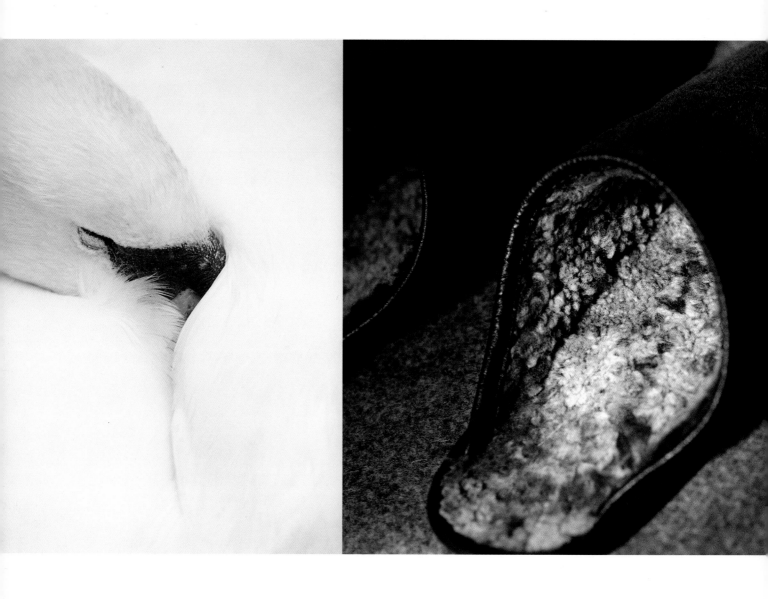

soft and hard Juxtaposing soft texture against hard can instantly redefine a room's atmosphere and purpose. Setting a pile of warm wool blankets on a bare wooden trunk adds a touch of comfort and familiarity; a hand-knotted rag rug hung over the side of an old enamel tub takes the chill out of the cold-looking surface. These are ways of counteracting a stark, minimalist interior and adding a sense of informality to an otherwise austere room. Simply draping a shawl over the back of an easy chair or placing a folded throw on the arm of a sofa can make the room look casual and inviting. Use these tricks whenever you need to, to make your home warm and welcoming.

above

Feathers invite you to stroke them – real swansdown was once used for making powder puffs and has lent its name to a thick soft fabric woven from wool mixed with silk, cotton or rayon. Tough suede slippers with a contrasting soft fleecy lining.

Slates arranged in a herringbone pattern have acquired a scattering of lichens. Snow blurs outlines and softens the landscape but also throws some elements into stark relief.

soft sculpture Nature does not grow in neat straight lines or perfectly formed shapes, but its imperfections and inconsistencies are part of its intrinsic attraction. Picture the gnarled trunk of a tree or the knobbly skins of potatoes dug from the ground; their natural flaws form interesting textural patterns. Similarly, in the traditional craft of knitting, different stitches are used to create a range of patterns in low relief. At its simplest, this might be the ribbing of a pair of thick socks. At the other end of the scale, Aran sweaters, the utility wear of the fishermen of the Aran Islands off the west coast of Ireland, reveal a wealth of complex patterns. Unlike the multi-coloured Fair Isle designs, true Aran knitting is confined to the natural colour of the fleece, relying solely on the intricacies of its sculptured surface for its impact. Some designs reflect the landscape and way of life – diagonal stitches across a purl panel represent winding cliff paths, while cable patterns relate to the fishermen's ropes. This is knitting at its most complex; for use in a modern home, the simplest patterns offer more scope. The wonderfully knobbly texture of garter stitch can be applied to cushion covers (see overleaf), and squares of different stitches can be made into bedcovers and throws.

knitted

cushion

covers

The simplest,

most basic of

knitting

stitches can

be used to

make cushion

covers that

will add

textural

interest and

bring a subtle

decorative

element to

any room.

To be sure of making a cushion cover that matches the measurements specified, it is advisable to check your tension before you begin knitting the cover itself. Knit a test square and compare it with the tension guides. If you have fewer stitches than given in the tension guide, use needles one size smaller than those recommended in the pattern. If you have more stitches than given in the tension guide, change to needles a size larger than specified.

Key to close-up of cushion covers pictured on the left: ridge pattern (top); double seed stitch (middle); garter stitch (bottom)

Ridge pattern cushion cover
The following pattern is for a 45cm (18in) square cushion cover.

materials

- *500gm Chunky wool*
- *1 pair 6½mm (No 3) needles*
- *45cm (18in) square cushion pad*

Tension guide: 14 stitches and 18 rows knitted in ridge pattern should measure 10cm (4in) square.

Cast on 65 stitches.
Work in ridge pattern as follows –
Row 1: Knit (right side)
Row 2: Purl
Repeat the above two rows twice.
Row 7: Knit
Row 8: Knit
These 8 rows form the pattern. Repeat until the length of the knitting measures twice the width. Cast off.
To finish, with right sides together, fold the

length of the knitting in half. Join the two halves of the cover together down the sides using neat back stitches. Gently press the seams under a damp cloth before turning the cover to the right side. Insert the cushion pad through the remaining open side, then slip stitch to close.

Garter stitch cushion cover

The following pattern is for a 50cm (20in) square cushion cover.

materials

- *500gm Aran wool*
- *1 pair 5mm (No 6) needles*

Tension guide: 18 stitches and 30 rows knitted in garter stitch should measure 10cm (4in) square.

Cast on 89 stitches.
Work in garter stitch (every row Knit) only. Continue until the length of the knitting measures twice its width. Cast off.
To finish, follow the instructions given for the ridge pattern cushion cover.

Double seed stitch cushion cover

The following pattern is for a 45cm (18in) square cover.

materials

- *300gm Double Knitting wool*
- *1 pair 4½mm (No 7) needles*

tension guide: 21 stitches and 32 rows knitted in double seed stitch should measure 10cm (4in) square.

Cast on 96 stitches.
Work in double seed stitch as follows:
Rows 1 and 2: *Knit 2, Purl 2, repeat from* to the end.
Rows 3 and 4: *Purl 2, Knit 2, repeat from* to the end.
These 4 rows form the pattern. Continue until the length of the knitting measures twice its width. Cast off.
To finish, follow the instructions given for the ridge pattern cover.

Garter stitch cushion cover with buttons

The following pattern is for a 50cm (20in) square cover.

materials

- *500gm Chunky wool*
- *1 pair 5½mm (No 5) needles*
- *4 buttons, 4cm (1½in) diameter*

Tension guide: 15 stitches and 26 rows knitted in garter stitch should measure 10cm (4in) square.

Cast on 74 stitches.
Work in garter stitch (every row Knit) only. Continue until the knitting measures 100cm (40in).
Work buttonholes over the next two rows:
Row 1: Knit 9. *cast off 5 stitches, Knit 12, repeat from* twice, cast off 5 stitches. Knit to the end.
Row 2: Knit, casting on 5 stitches above those cast off in the previous row.
Continue in garter stitch for a further 5cm (2in).
To finish, follow the ridge pattern cover instructions, but use buttons to close.

left

A cushion cover knitted in garter stitch using brown chunky wool has large wooden buttons to fasten it. As well as allowing the easy removal of the cover for washing, they add both decorative and textural detail.

taming texture As the landscape changes with the seasons, so its visible texture alters. A ridged ploughed field, with a charming wiggle or two that betrays the human presence behind the machine, translates into a cushion cover knitted in a thick ribbed stitch, an armchair upholstered in robust corduroy or a rug woven in stripes. Rows of fringing or individual tufted stitches like permanent tailor's tacks could represent the emerging tender seedlings. The use of texture to embellish a plain material has a long tradition in the home – knitting, quilting a lightly padded fabric or self-coloured embroidery all create three-dimensional interest. Fabrics gain decorative appeal without relying on the intrusive use of colour.

A crude trough hewn from a massive block of timber, gnarled and cracked with age, brings texture to a simply furnished hallway and also serves a useful purpose keeping shoes tidy.

left

*A worn Welsh
blanket, cut
down to size and
backed with felt
plus strips of
non-slip matting,
makes an elegant
rug for a hallway
and softens a
somewhat
austere setting.*

65

elemental textures Sometimes a two-dimensional pattern on a favourite piece of pottery or decorative metalware can be the inspiration for a three-dimensional texture. Here, the painted lines on a rustic glazed earthenware bowl have been translated into thick lines of cord threaded through a coarse open-weave fabric (turn the page for full instructions). On the original bowl, the shiny glaze reflects the light and adds extra interest; on the textured fabric the light passes right through and adds to the design. As a painted wrought-iron table becomes weathered by the elements, it gains an extra textural dimension. A combination of flaking paint and rust produces extra tones of colour and texture that help it blend easily into a garden setting.

above

A painted wrought-iron garden table weathered to an authentic-looking antiquity gains in texture and interest. Lines of cord threaded through coarsely woven banana fibre mimic the crude stripes of an earthenware peasant bowl – just one example of the way in which pattern can be an inspiration for texture; the introduction of fabric offers new textural opportunities.

embroidered vase
cover

Inspired by the
colours and graphic
pattern of an old,
ceramic peasant
bowl, this
sculptural vase
cover is made from
a stiff, loosely
woven material
traditionally used
in hat-making, and
embroidered with
simple running
stitches in
plaited cord.

materials

The following instructions can be used to make a cover to fit any size of cylindrical glass vase.

- *banana fibre*
- *3mm (⅛in) wide plaited cord in two different colours*
- *tapestry needle*

1 Measure the height and the circumference of your vase, and cut out a piece of banana fibre to size, adding 7.5cm (3in) to each dimension. This extra fabric is included for ease of fit as well as for making a seam – it is important that the cover does not fit too tightly around the vase. Use the circumference measurement along a selvedge to make the lower edge of the cover.

2 To calculate the amount of cord required, plan the number of rows of stitching you would like to make and in what colour sequence. I placed the rows 2.5cm (1in) apart and used the two colours randomly. For each row of stitching, allow the height of your vase and an additional 13cm (5in). Multiply this figure by the number of rows you have planned to make.

3 Cut the cord into the required lengths. Knot one end of each length and, using the tapestry needle, loosely work vertical lines of running stitch from the base edge of the vase cover to the top. For the final row of stitching, fold under 1.5cm (⅝in) along the two side edges. Overlap the folded edges a little and work the

stitches through all the layers to join the fabric and form a tube. Knot the cord ends at the top of the vase cover, and trim any excess cord.

4 Place the vase cover over the vase and gently push down. This will distort the straight lines of stitching into gentle curves. If you wish, fray the top edge of the vase cover.

Texture notes

You can try using different textured threads to make alternative vase covers. String, coarse wool or other types of cord would be effective, but avoid using threads that are excessively thick, otherwise you will distort the weave of the fabric too much.

Rather than making vertical lines of running stitches, they could be placed horizontally or even used in combination to create a simple grid pattern.

Try experimenting with fraying the top edge of the cover. When cutting out the banana fibre, allow greater height than specified and fray the top edge to allow the fibres to extend like plant tendrils around the top of the vase. The stiffness of the fabric means that they can be sculpted upwards rather than just flopping outwards.

This technique could be applied on a much larger scale, to make blinds or screens instead of lace or muslin curtains. Wonderful patterns would be created on the walls as the light passes through.

age-old patinas Texture that comes with age is one of the most enviable forms of decoration. Years of polishing combined with everyday use – and, it has to be said, a fair amount of dirt – give wood a depth that is nearly impossible to fake but easy to destroy through over-zealous restoration. The treads of a stone or wooden staircase worn into a dip from the passage of many feet have an appeal that cannot be copied. Paintwork that is showing signs of age is much easier to imitate, to bring an air of antiquity to a room or a piece of furniture. Techniques such as crackle glazing can age new woodwork instantly, while layering paint on wooden furniture and then rubbing back the top coat on handles, doors – wherever wear occurs naturally – simulates a genuine 'distressed' finish. Mottled, pigmented plaster can be achieved with modern distempers and many paint companies produce 'heritage' ranges of colours based on traces of paint discovered in period houses.

You can also introduce an element of weathering or antiquity into an otherwise new interior simply by making a feature of a collection of sea-smoothed pebbles or giving an attractively faded and worn rug pride of place on the floor.

the rough with the smooth Pairing rough textures with smooth illustrates just how much effect texture has on colour. Smooth, light-reflecting surfaces enhance a colour and give it added impact; rough, matt surfaces add patches of shadow and differing depths of colour. A piece of olive silk, for example, shimmers attractively; the same shade on an unglazed cotton may look positively drab. Velvet refracts the light at angles and creates different tones, while rough hessian allows light through.

From the pairing of a handful of shiny mother-of-pearl buttons in a roughly lined box comes the idea of combining rough unbleached linen and delicate broderie anglaise to create a pretty two-sided curtain – see following pages for instructions.

above

Look for inspiration in the tiniest details. Nothing is too insignificant to contribute an idea for the modern country home, from the juxtaposition of smooth buttons against a rough box to matt-textured eggs in a roughly woven nest.

A row of dishcloths hung out to dry can suggest a rustic café curtain or an easy way to make a wall hanging, using rope and even wooden pegs themselves to hold up a length of fabric.

linen and

lace curtain

Two contrasting

traditional country

fabrics – coarse

unbleached linen

and ultra-feminine

and refined

broderie anglaise –

are combined

to make a

texturally lively

curtain. It can be

looped back to

one side or the

other by tying the

bottom ties to

one of the buttons

sewn on to the

linen.

materials

- *lace fabric*
- *unbleached linen fabric*
- *120cm (48in) of 1.5 cm (⅝in) wide cotton tape*
- *sewing thread*
- *10 cream buttons*

1 Measure the width of the window and then the length, from the point from which you wish to hang the curtain to the windowsill.

2 Cut both the lace and linen to size, adding a 1.5cm (⅝in) seam allowance all round. Cut the cotton tape into 4 equal lengths for ties.

3 With the linen right side up, fold each tie in half (end to end) and place one at each corner 7.5cm (3in) from the raw side edges with the fold aligning with the top or bottom raw edges and the ties extending inwards down the fabric parallel to the side edges. Pin, then baste in position. Sew a row of evenly spaced buttons in line with the ties down each side of the curtain.

4 With right sides together, place the lace over the linen, aligning the raw edges. Pin, baste, then machine stitch together along the top, bottom and one side edge, taking a 1.5cm (⅝in) seam allowance. Trim the corners. Turn right side out, press, then slip stitch the side edge to close.

5 Tie the curtain to two small hooks fixed either side of the window.

a soft touch Soft fabrics bring a sensuous touch to the modern country home, and nowhere more so than in the bedroom. A room may look abstemious and pared-down, but by introducing luxury through textiles a simple setting becomes comfortable to live in. In a plain bedroom, a down-filled eiderdown or a cable-stitched blanket, for example, is the perfect counterpart to a severe iron bedstead. Degrees of softness, from feathery seedheads to furry buds, are perfectly demonstrated in nature. The gently abrasive bristles of a field of barley might be reinterpreted as raw unbleached linen; the soft curls of old man's beard might inspire a fine pashmina shawl or throw and furry thick-piled pussy willow, a pair of extravagant velvet slippers.

above

Although feathers are soft, they are surprisingly resilient – and waterproof, too. Long, bristly barley whiskers look soft and feathery from a distance, while pussy willow flowers are velvet-tipped and eminently strokable. Old man's beard is much more appealing than its name suggests: the seeds with their densely plumed 'tails' are as soft as teased and carded wool.

eiderdown

A generous feather
and down-filled
eiderdown brings
warmth, comfort
and a country feel
to a sparse modern
bedroom. It is made
using traditional
lawn dress fabrics
– a tiny lilac
sprigged design
combined with
a coordinating
plain fabric.

materials

The following quantities are for making an eiderdown measuring 140 x 160cm (56 x 63in) to fit a standard double bed.

- *3.3m (3¾yd) of 145cm (57in) wide cotton downproof lining fabric*
- *1.8m (2yd) of 140cm (44in) wide cotton floral fabric*
- *4m (4yd) of 155cm (60in) wide plain cotton fabric*
- *6.2m (6¾yd) piping cord*
- *sewing thread*
- *feather and down filling*

note You can either use new feather and down or filling collected from old pillows and eiderdowns.

1 From the lining fabric, cut out two rectangles each measuring 143 x 163cm (57¼ x 65¼in). This includes a 1.5cm (⅝in) seam allowance.

2 For the front of the eiderdown, cut out 4 strips from the floral fabric and 3 strips from the plain fabric, each strip measuring 23 x 163cm (9¼in x 65¼in). For the back of the eiderdown, cut out a rectangle from the plain fabric measuring 143 x 163cm (57¼ x 65¼in). All these measurements include a 1.5cm (⅝in) seam allowance.

3 Cut the remaining plain fabric into bias strips wide enough to cover the piping cord comfortably, allowing an additional 1.5cm (⅝in) seam allowance. Machine sew as many strips together end to end to cover the whole length of the piping cord. With wrong sides together, fold the bias strip in

half down its length around the piping cord. Pin, baste, then machine stitch along the length of the bias strip to enclose the cord. Lay the plain eiderdown back on a flat surface right side up. Lay the piping all the way round the edge of the fabric, aligning the outside raw edges of the piping case and the eiderdown back. Pin, baste, then machine stitch in place, taking a 1.5cm (⅝in) seam allowance.

4 For the eiderdown front, with right sides together, pin, then machine stitch the fabric strips together down the long edges, taking a 1.5cm (⅝in) seam allowance, alternating the floral and plain fabrics. Press the seams open. The eiderdown front should now be the same size as the back and the two lining pieces.

5 Lay one lining piece on a flat surface and place the eiderdown back right side up on top. Place the eiderdown front right side down on top of the back, then finally add the second lining piece. Make sure that all the raw edges align. Pin, baste, then machine stitch all the layers together along the two longer edges and one shorter edge. Trim the corners for a neat finish. Turn the eiderdown right side out and press.

6 Lay the eiderdown right side up on a flat surface. Pin, baste, then machine stitch all four layers of fabric together along each strip seam line, forming 7 channels.

7 Fill each channel with feather and down filling, distributing it evenly. Be careful not to overfill, otherwise the eiderdown will be too dense and puffed up. Close the open edge with neat slip stitches.

pattern & plain

Pattern can be subtle and understated or it can be bold and vibrant; both have a place in modern country style. Nature is an almost inexhaustible inspiration for pattern, much of it beautiful and all of it purposeful: speckles and spots on petals guide bees straight to the flower's nectar; vivid stripes on a caterpillar warn off predators. The striations on snail shells become part of a larger design when grouped together and even the plainest roof tiles form a rhythmic pattern en masse.

mix and match There is a long and honourable tradition of mixing patterned fabrics and plain colours in the country home. Today, the most familiar combinations are pretty florals with fresh gingham checks or utilitarian ticking – once an undercover fabric for mattresses and pillow casings, but now appreciated for its stylish stripes.

In this cottage bedroom, there is a rather more ambitious combination of random and formal patterns, though quite unself-consciously achieved. The patchwork quilt is a haphazard assortment of printed and plain fabrics, assembled with barely any thought for tone or pattern, forming a brilliant kaleidoscope of coloured cottons. In contrast, the chintz curtains at the window have a formal design with a recognizable repeat to the pattern. Chintz is a fabric more usually associated with grander houses and the curtains were probably antique shop finds, cut down and adapted to do service in the bedroom. Yet because the room is relatively simply furnished and the curtains hang without ostentation from modest poles, there is no clash of fabrics or designs. The quilt and curtains supply all the detail in the room and the shiny plaster walls and bare floorboards form a plain, neutral backdrop.

linear undertones Graphic patterns are valuable for their strong impact. Think of the sharply defined furrows of a ploughed field, a stone wall snaking across the landscape or the solid bars of a farm gate, which can be reinterpreted as striped fabrics or simply as a line of stitching punctuating plain fabric. But graphics can be subtle, too. Rigid grid-based patterns can be blurred and softened to make them less immediately obvious. The roughcast stone wall in the picture is composed of horizontal and vertical elements but weather and time have taken their toll, making the overall pattern subtle. Only close scrutiny reveals the underlying structure. Just as you would use a splash of contrasting colour to break up an unbroken expanse of a single shade, so you can introduce another pattern to interrupt the monotony of a regularly repeating graphic design. The lifebelt hanging from a nail on the stone wall is an unintentional example of using a device to punctuate the basic grid of the background. And you can use this principle in the home. The rug on the following pages is studded with a series of toggles that interrupt the rigid pattern of the fabric – the padding, too, curves the lines of the pattern and makes them less formal.

padded rug

Looking like a mini eiderdown, this plump rug is made in checked fabric and backed with heavy glazed, raincoat-style cotton. Tiny rolls of leather tied with cord are used both to decorate the rug as well as to give it extra shape. This rug could be used equally well for an occasional picnic.

materials

To make a 140cm (56in) square rug
■ *1.5m (1½yd) of 145cm (56in) wide checked wool fabric*
■ *1.5m (1½yd) of 145cm (56in) wide glazed, heavy cotton (used for raincoats)*
■ *1.5m (1½yd) of 90cm (36in) wide hounds-tooth checked wool fabric*
■ *medium-weight polyester wadding*
■ *sewing thread*
■ *brown cord or brown shoe laces*
■ *piece of brown leather 26cm (10¼in) square*
■ *pair of pinking shears*
■ *long, large-eyed darning needle*

1 For the front of the rug, mark out a 137cm (55in) square on the checked wool fabric, making sure that the pattern is symmetrically arranged within the square. Repeat with the glazed cotton fabric for the rug back. Cut out both squares.

2 For the rug binding, mark out 4 strips on the hounds-tooth checked fabric – 2 measuring 137 x 9cm (55 x 3½in), the other 2 measuring 143 x 9cm (57 x 3½in), all including seam allowances. Cut out.

3 Lay the rug back right side down on a flat surface. Place the wadding on top and cut to fit the fabric. With right side up, position the rug front on top, aligning the edges all round. Pin, then baste the layers together.

4 Take the two longer strips of binding, turn 1.5cm (⅝in) to the wrong side all round, then press. Repeat with the remaining strips, but leave the short ends as they are. Fold all 4 strips in half down their length, right side out. Press well.

5 Place one of the shorter folded strips along one edge of the rug, overlapping the raw edges of the rug front and back with the folded edges of the strip. Baste, then machine stitch in place through all the layers of fabric, wadding and binding. Repeat with the remaining shorter folded strip and the opposite edge of the rug. Repeat the process with the two longer pieces of binding and the remaining rug edges, encasing the raw edges of the rug and the ends of the first two strips of binding.

6 Using a tape measure and pins, plan the positioning of leather toggles. These are arranged in a grid of 4 rows, each row consisting of 4 toggles. Position the first pin in one corner of the rug, 27cm (10½in) from both the top and side rug edges. Moving across the rug to the other side and keeping the toggles in a straight line, position the next 3 toggles 29cm (11½in) apart. Mark the next 3 lines of toggles, with 29cm (11½in) between the rows.

7 Cut the cord into 20cm (8in) lengths. From the leather, cut out 16 pieces, each measuring 6.5cm (2½in) square, with pinking shears. For each toggle, thread the needle with a length of cord. At the position marked, pass the needle through the rug to the wrong side, leaving about 7.5cm (3in) of cord protruding from the rug front. Make a short stitch, then bring the needle and thread back to the rug front. Roll up a leather square, place between the two cord ends and knot the cord to secure. Trim the excess cord if required.

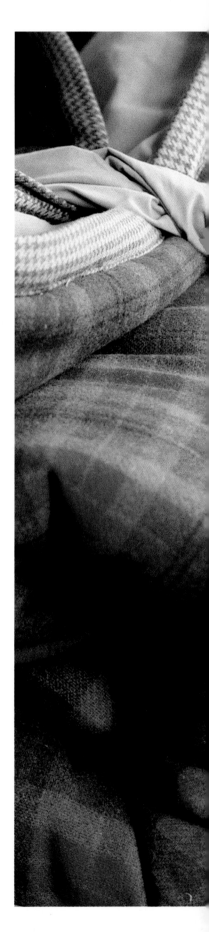

lateral thinking Here are two subtle patterns used to good effect within the home. A thinly padded seat for a rustic bench is made from a typically understated Scots tweed and a plump cushion with a cover knitted in a lacy stitch. An original 1940s knitting pattern for a cardigan provided the design for the cushion cover: adapting it by using bigger needles and thicker yarn has not only made it more robust for everyday use but has changed the original effect of the stitch, making the ribbing more prominent. Thinking laterally and using something intended for one purpose for another quite different project is one of the keys to creating an interesting and unusual home. Another idea along the same lines would be to use a traditional smocking stitch in an unconventional way: to gather a curtain, for example.

While the pattern of the knitted cushion cover is created by the twisting of yarn around needles, the patterning of the tweed is achieved by the subtle mixing of colour. Just like heather on moorland, which from a distance is little more than a purple haze, up close it reveals something more defined and quite different. Scattered among the simple checked weave of the tweed are wonderful flecks of green and rust.

repeat performance One of the easiest ways to build up pattern is to use repeating

blocks. Some images in the countryside immediately suggest repeat patterns: neatly

stacked logs in the woodshed, the layers of a dry-stone wall, ripples on the sand left

by the receding tide. Closer to home, you can find repeat patterns in a woven basket,

a wicker chair or the panes of a lattice window. All of these patterns are built up from

smaller units, in much the same way that traditional sewing skills such as appliqué and

patchwork use individual pieces of fabric to build a design. On the following pages you

will find instructions for creating a border for a tablecloth, built up from scraps of

patterned fabric cut into rectangles, then appliquéd to the cloth.

above

Look beyond the alarming image of scorched earth and the fractured clay produces a pattern that is entirely random yet composed of recognizably similar shapes. A dry-stone wall made from layers of rounded rocks and flat slabs offers a lesson in building up a repeat pattern from irregular elements. The pleasing symmetry of a basket woven from split cane is broken up by the range of tones.

appliquéd

tablecloth and

tablemats

In true modern-

country style,

plain table linen

is patterned with

restraint.

Using the traditional

art of appliqué in

its simplest form,

remnants of old

cotton dress fabrics

in tiny floral and

abstract prints

create a graphic

border on a

tablecloth and

corner details on

a set of tablemats.

materials

For each mat

■ *4 rectangular pieces of patterned cotton fabric, each measuring 12.5 x 10cm (5 x 4in)*
■ *2 rectangular pieces of plain cotton or linen fabric, each measuring 32 x 45cm (13 x 18in)*
■ *sewing thread*

note Use one or two patterned fabrics or a different pattern for each corner.

For the tablecoth

■ *a ready-made plain cotton or linen tablecloth, or plain cotton or linen fabric cut and hemmed to the required size*
■ *remnants of patterned cotton fabric*
■ *sewing thread*

To make the mats

1 Lay each patterned fabric piece on a flat surface, right side down. With two of the fabric pieces, turn the left-hand short edge and the bottom edge 1.5cm (⅝in) to the wrong side. Press well. With the remaining two pieces, turn the right-hand short edge and the top edge 1.5cm (⅝in) to the wrong side, and press.

2 Lay one of the plain pieces of fabric on a flat surface, right side up. Position a patterned piece of fabric, right side up, at each corner, aligning the raw edges with the raw edges of the mat. Pin the patterned fabric pieces in place along the folded edges only, then machine stitch in place, working the stitches close to the folded edges.

3 With right sides together, pin the remaining plain piece of fabric to the mat

front. Machine stitch along three edges, taking a 1.5cm (⅝in) seam allowance. Trim the corners close to the stitching line to reduce the excess fabric. Turn the mat right side out. Turn in the raw edges of the opening and slip stitch to close. Press the mat thoroughly.

To make the tablecloth

1 Choose two opposite edges of the tablecloth for appliquéing with a border, according to how the fabric falls on the table. From the fabric remnants, mark and cut out enough rectangular pieces to form two equally sized strips, the same length as the chosen tablecloth edges, adding a 1.5cm (⅝in) allowance all round each piece, for seams and hemming. All the remnant pieces should measure the same height, but you may wish to vary the widths slightly to create a less regular look.
For this tablecloth, I cut each remnant piece 15 x 12.5cm (6 x 5in).

2 Arrange the patterned pieces in 2 lines. When you are satisfied with both arrangements, with right sides together, pin the pieces together down the sides to form 2 strips. Taking a 1.5cm (⅝in) seam allowance, machine stitch together, and press the seams open.

3 Turn the two long edges and the two ends of each strip 1.5 cm (⅝in) to the wrong side and press. Pin the strips in position across the opposite edges of the tablecloth, placing the lower edge of each strip 7.5cm (3in) from the hemmed edge of the tablecloth. Machine stitch the strips in place, working the stitches close to the folded edges.

natural order The obvious way to introduce pattern to a room is to use textiles – rugs, curtains, cushions and upholstery. But in some situations fabrics are far from suitable, particularly in a damp or humid bathroom. Painted patterns will stand up to moisture and wear if you choose the correct formula paint before going ahead. Geometric shapes are the easiest to draw: rulers, masking tape and a builder's set square will help you get angles and straight lines spot on. Or use contrasting colour tiles on the floor and the walls, especially in a shower area. You may have to rely on the architecture of the room itself to provide pattern: the vertical lines of tongue-and-groove panelling or even the regular stripes of painted wooden floorboards.

far left

Natural geometry at work. Much-magnified triangular crystals of frost on blades of grass are themselves composed of smaller branching crystals

left

Geometric pattern in action. Bold tiles are laid differently on the walls and floor in a simple pared down bathroom. Even the tongue-and-groove panelling and the floorboards form part of the overall design, adding pattern and interest to the room.

humble origins Stripes are a furnishing classic. But these are not the bold stripes of

a Regency sofa or drawing-room wallpaper; modern country makes use of stripes with

far more modest origins. Ticking is a fabric traditionally used for pillows and mattresses:

it is a robust cotton twill, closely woven to prevent scratchy feather stubs from piercing

the fabric. Nowadays, we appreciate it as much for its interesting, often intricately

woven, stripes as well as its tough, hard-wearing qualities. Another traditional striped

fabric is humble shirting: not the fine materials used for smart office shirts, but the

wonderfully thick and hard-wearing cotton of workwear and nightshirts. While ticking

is best for covering chairs and sofas, shirting fabric is much softer and drapes more

readily. The cushions on the previous pages are sewn from shirting fabrics, which are

often striped in blues and greys with a touch of red or brown. Shirting and ticking can

be mixed and matched, united by their stripes or colour.

in full bloom Floral patterns have been used in country homes for hundreds of years and it's easy to see why, as inspiration is all around – from the cottage garden to hedgerows and fields. The flowers in a garden are the perfect starting point for your own ideas. Looking at different plants will help you decide whether you prefer delicate sprigged patterns, big bold blooms, random mixtures of flowers or adjoining strands of harmonizing – or clashing – colours. Even a single plant can suggest a multiplicity of patterns, from a filigree of green leaves to the markings on a petal. Individual flowers might inspire different moods: simple, open blooms suggest a light, carefree style, while others, intricately formed and complex, hint at mystery and drama.

above

Garden flowers offer
valuable guidance on
all aspects of pattern
and colour. The intense
purple of a hardy
geranium flower (far
left) is striated with
veins of darker and
lighter colour. Deep
purple russian sage
and clematis flowers
are lifted by fluffy pink

clouds of thalictrum.
Penstemon flowers,
show the striped honey
guides that lead bees
to the nectaries.
Adding white to a
medley of greens adds
light and clarity in a
garden or a room.

right

Turning tradition on its head gives a new slant on fabrics. For example, a single antique curtain printed with peony-like flowers has been given new life as a bedspread, while the curtains proper are stitched from shirting fabric. A length of ticking has been used to make a headboard cover – see page 45 for instructions. The cushion covers were sewn from early twentieth-century farmer's neckerchiefs, backed with a modern check.

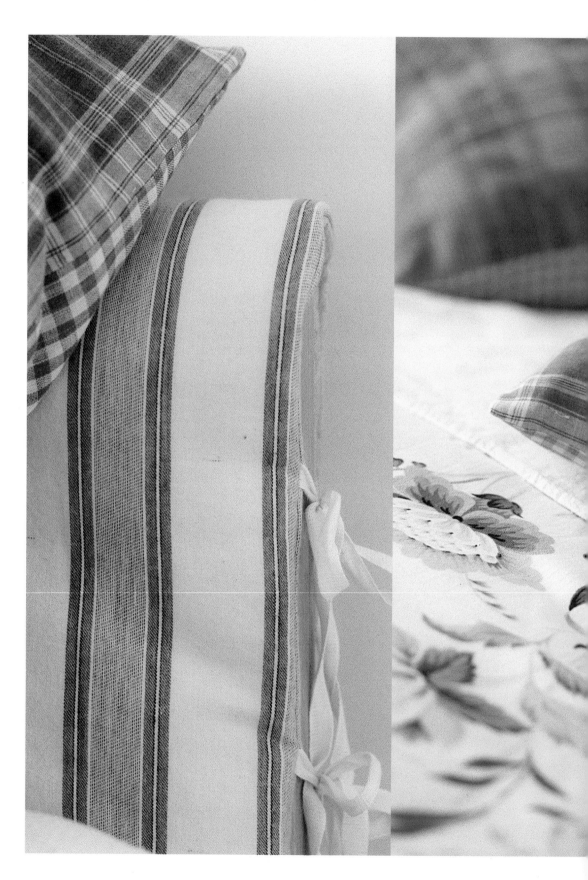

floral arrangements Just as in real life, printed flowers come in a vast array, from

small sprigged patterns to vast painterly splashes of petals on a larger-than-life scale.

Once again, you can turn to the garden for help in combining different floral fabrics.

Look at plants growing side by side and you'll be able to assess whether tiny starry

flowers – translated into a small sprigged pattern – will complement bold brash blooms

– in the guise of an equally bold print fabric – or lose out altogether. You will also gain

valuable experience of which colours look well together. If you feel uncertain whether

the floral fabrics you plan to use complement each other, then try linking them by

making sure they have a colour in common, or using the same style of trimming on both.

above

A floral fabric printed entirely in shades of green is an elegant alternative to a busy print in all the colours of the flower garden. These cushion covers illustrate the successful mixing of two different patterns – one with painterly blooms, the other a tiny sprig design – both printed in shades of complementary green. The different scale of motif forms a necessary contrast, while the muted shades of green mirror glaucous hostas or purple-grey sage.

atmosphere

As every romantic knows, creating the right atmosphere is crucial. One essential is good lighting: it's impossible to feel relaxed in the full glare of a100 watt bulb. Similarly, a low winter sun blazing in across the table at lunch or tea time can be extremely uncomfortable. Textiles can play a large part: sometimes all that's needed is a length of sheer muslin or an antique linen sheet hanging at the window to filter the light. If you have shutters at your windows, a panel of sheer organza gives extra privacy during daylight. More drastic measures are sometimes needed: nothing less than blackout curtains will do if you want to discourage small children from waking too early. Cosy, padded curtains are an advantage in draughty rooms and can make a noticeable difference to the temperature.

above

Leaving windows
uncurtained will make
you aware of how
daylight changes with
the seasons, from the
clear light of spring
to the mellow haze of
summer. At certain
angles, every lump and
loving imperfection in
roughly plastered walls
is thrown into relief.

In this room, the
windows are a focal
point; adding curtains
or blinds would
detract from their
architectural merit.
A medieval hallway is
suffused with a
cheerful burst of
summer sun that
bleaches out the
flagstones' detail.

light relief As the seasons change, so does the quality of light. In winter the sun is low and weak; as spring progresses it gains in intensity, so that by the time summer arrives daylight is at its strongest and richest. The quality of light affects the way in which we see colours: summer light is tempered with heat and creates a hazy effect, whereas in winter colours seem pin sharp. The room pictured (above left and centre) has been left uncurtained deliberately so that its atmosphere changes with the seasons. In spring, the light slanting through the windows is cold and clean and the whitewashed walls are icily pure. In summer, the sun's rays turn the walls a mellow cream, while autumn sunsets colour them a warm pink.

simple serenity Tranquillity is an elusive quality, difficult to define and even harder to create without all the proper elements being in place. To create a restful atmosphere, a room must be light and airy, with no superfluous detail and no harsh colours. Choose pale, muted colours, fabrics in plain tones or understated patterns and simple, unadorned furniture to make a room feel calm and peaceful. The bedroom pictured here epitomizes tranquillity: the light is soft and suffused; and the walls painted a gentle white reflect it still further. Using a pale woodwash to colour the cupboards softens the wood but leaves a hint of the natural grain visible. Extra light filters through from a window in an adjacent room and will have lost any harshness it may have had before reaching the bedroom.

To create a tranquil retreat, you must be ruthless and strip back a room to the barest essentials, so that every piece of furniture has a function and every paint colour, every scrap of textile and upholstery contributes to the atmosphere without adding extraneous and distracting detail. As daylight fades, the best lighting to add is candlelight, with its gentle warm glow and flickering shadows.

left

Sheer muslin curtains that shift with every passing breeze say summer is here. Once again, pale colours on the walls and floor reinforce the light, airy atmosphere and the day bed is dressed in the plainest of stripes. For a successful decorating scheme for a restful room, you need only remember that simplicity equals serenity.

bright ideas On a large expanse of window, breaking blinds up into individual elements gives you far more control over the light coming into the room. Much as we love sunlight, shade is important for comfort, and using a trio of blinds allows you to block an errant shaft of light without screening the whole window. Using coarsely woven fabrics in bright colours changes the colour of the light cast into the room – bright oranges and reds can be used to boost the sun's intensity on gloomier days. Late afternoon sun, particularly towards the end of the year, makes shockingly bright midsummer colours seem richer and mellower, with no hint of brashness – like the beach huts above, on fire with colour as the sun goes down.

earthy palette Colour helps create atmosphere, and these pictures illustrate the warm inviting glow of earth tones and pigments. An old rendered wall, patched and painted for practical reasons, has acquired an attractive colour scheme quite by chance, the soft pink and red tones further defined by the hard edges of the window frame. The same warm pinky terracotta is repeated indoors, in the kitchen, with hand-made tiles for a splashback and a lampshade that picks up the colour higher up. Even the casually placed tea towel contributes to the scheme. The kitchen may look rustic and simple, but it has been carefully thought through. It conforms to standard design principles and all the elements are there, just reduced to their simplest form. For example, the sink is close to the window for maximum daylight, backed up by a practical pendant lamp. On the following pages, a similar contrast between the hard lines and soft colours of the cottage wall has been created using soft rich red webbing to repair a folding wooden patio chair. The contrast between coloured webbing and the graphic lines of the frame repeats the effect. When summer is over, the chair, with its strong, appealing colour, could easily become part of the indoor furniture.

jute-seated

fold-up chair

Revamp an

attractively

weathered

garden chair

with bright

webbing and

bring a splash

of colour to

the garden at

the same time.

If you want to

be really

clever, add

accent notes

by using

ribbon

markers for

rows of seeds.

materials

- ▦ *5m (5½yd) of 5cm (2in) wide brown jute upholstery webbing (available plain or, as used here, with a contrasting line down the centre)*
- ▦ *pair of rubber gloves*
- ▦ *1 pack red hand dye*
- ▦ *250g (8oz) salt*
- ▦ *wooden fold-up director's chair*
- ▦ *pair of pliers*
- ▦ *upholstery tacks or staples*
- ▦ *hammer*

1 Wash the webbing thoroughly and leave damp. Wearing rubber gloves, dissolve the dye in 1 litre (2¼ pints) of warm water. Pour 6 litres (13 pints) of very hot tap water into a bowl or bucket. Add the salt, stirring well, then add the dye solution and stir again.

2 Put the unfolded damp webbing into the bowl or bucket and leave for at least an hour. Make sure the webbing is totally submerged in the dye solution and agitate occasionally, particularly during the first 15 minutes of the process.

3 Remove the webbing from the dye solution and rinse in cold water until the water runs clear, then wash in hot, soapy water. Rinse well and allow to dry.

4 If the chair is an old one, strip off all the existing fabric seating, using pliers to remove any tacks from the frame. Using a tape measure and pencil, mark the position of the webbing strips – 6 pieces for the chair seat and 3 for the chair back, the first strips positioned close to the top of the chair back. Make sure that the strips are evenly spaced.

5 Turn under 2cm (¾in) along one short end of the length of webbing. Position it at the first pencil mark on one side of the seat frame, then turn the chair upside-down and secure the webbing, hem side down, to the underside of the seat frame with 3 tacks or staples positioned close to the fold. Turn the chair upright. With the seat frame open, pull the webbing as tight as possible across the frame to the same position on the opposite side. Cut the webbing to the required length, adding an extra 2cm (¾in) for turning under. Make a note of the length. Fold up the seat frame halfway, turn the chair upside-down and tack or staple the webbing, hem side down as before, to the opposite side of the seat frame. It is much easier to hammer the tacks into the frame when the chair is half closed rather than fully open. Cut 5 more strips of webbing to the same length as the first and attach to complete the seat.

6 Cut and attach 3 webbing strips to the frame of the chair back in the same way. As you can see from the photograph (top right), the turned ends of the webbing are placed on the inside edge of the corner struts, so that the webbing then wraps around the outside and across the front of the struts.

Dappled light from the sun shining through a tree is refracted further by frosted and etched panels of glass. A powerful source of light, coupled with a magnifying lens, is crucial to revealing the perfect, sculptural structure of a dandelion seedhead.

A blind of coarse, dark canvas cuts off the view: it imposes its own horizon and subdues the mood inside the room.

mood swings By controlling the light within a room, you can alter the room's atmosphere, and use light – and shade – to dramatic effect. Thick heavy curtains against streaming light create an arresting combination of light and dark, like a painterly chiaroscuro, while a blind in a sombre colour creates a dramatic horizon and correspondingly moody atmosphere. A panel of frosted glass is a permanent version of muslin hung at a window and creates a diffuse source of light. Direct light is best at highlighting a single object – a spotlight focused on a piece of sculpture or 'found art' will reveal every detail. Reflected light is more subtle and relies on pale walls and ceiling to bounce rays back and illuminate the room indirectly.

canopy

This garden

canopy gently

screens the glare

from the sun in old-

fashioned style.

It is made from an

aging piece of jute

suspended from

four poles, held in

position with

ordinary garden

umbrella stands –

dispensing with the

need for guy ropes.

In this way, the

canopy can be easily

resited in the garden

as the sun moves

round during the day.

materials

■ 4½m (4yd) of 1m (1yd) wide
loose-weave jute

■ 4 wooden poles, minimum
length 1.8m (6ft)

■ 4 plastic garden umbrella stands

■ at least 2m (80in) rope

■ fabric for the canopy

■ 4 x 12mm (½in) diameter
metal eyelets (optional)

■ 4 hooks

■ 2m (80in) woven cotton tape

note When choosing poles, it is important
to select ones that fit tightly into the
umbrella stands. If the poles are slightly too
thick, shave the bases with a sharp knife
until they fit. For the canopy fabric, you can
either use a ready-hemmed piece of old
fabric, such as jute used here, or cut a
piece of canvas fabric to size and hem. The
amount of fabric required depends on the
size of canopy you want.

1 Cut the fabric into 4 pieces, each 1m
(1yd) square. Insert the poles into the

stands, making sure that they are pushed well in and firmly secure. Place an umbrella stand in the centre of one piece of jute and gather up the fabric around the stand. Wind a length of rope neatly around the base of the pole and the gathered fabric (see the photograph above), and tie the ends in a knot to secure. Trim the excess fabric above the rope binding. Repeat for the remaining stands.

2 Hem the canopy fabric, if required. Fix an eyelet at each corner of the canopy

fabric, according to the manufacturer's instructions.

3 Insert a hook into each pole about 5cm (2in) from the top. To suspend the canopy, slip each hook through an eyelet. For a purely decorative effect, cut the cotton tape into 4 equal lengths, thread one through each eyelet and tie in a knot or bow. An alternative way of suspending the canopy would be to omit the eyelets and stitch a length of cotton tape directly onto the fabric at each corner.

candles in

containers

A variety of everyday containers can be adapted and used as decorative candleholders, including metal tins, glass jars and even teacups, as long as they are watertight and heat-resistant. As the candles burn, the molten wax is literally contained.

materials

- *container*
- *wire- or paper-cored wick*
(available from craft suppliers)
- *wick sustainer*
(available from craft suppliers)
- *pair of pliers*
- *wooden skewer, thin stick or pencil*
- *paraffin wax (available from craft*
suppliers in blocks or easy-to-melt granules)
- *double boiler*

note Wicks are available in three widths:
small for containers up to 5cm (2in)
diameter, medium for containers 5-10cm
(2-4in) diameter and large for containers
10-15cm (4-6in) diameter.

1 Make sure that your chosen container
is clean and completely dry.

2 Cut a length of wick approximately 5cm
(2in) deeper than the container. Thread a
wick sustainer onto one end of the length of
wick, and tighten the hole with pliers. Drop
the sustainer and wick into the centre of
the container. Tie the other end of the wick
loosely to a wooden skewer, thin stick or
pencil placed centrally across the top of
the container (see the photograph). The
wick should be straight but not taut.

3 Gently heat the wax in the top of a
double boiler. Once the wax has melted,
carefully pour it into the container. Leave to
cool at room temperature. The wax starts
to set from the bottom upwards, and as it
cools, a slight dip will appear in the centre.
Fill the dip with more hot wax until the
surface is level. When set, trim the wick.

ever-changing atmosphere Light has such power to alter a colour and thus the atmosphere – that's why you often find people struggling towards the windows of a department store with an armful of different coloured garments or poring over hanks of wool or embroidery thread outside the door of a crafts shop. Pink walls can change from the colour of newly applied plaster to apricot over the course of the day, for example. Magenta can seem shockingly close to red at midday, then fade towards violet as evening draws on. So when choosing colours for walls, furniture and fabrics, you should always bear in mind at what time of day a room is going to be most used. In a bedroom that is also an evening retreat, you can use rich colours with impunity, safe in the knowledge that they will be softened by pools of light from carefully sited table lamps or even candlelight. Gold, ochre, blue with a touch of red added until it veers towards purple, are all strong shades enhanced by evening light and candlelight.

inviting glow Though central heating has theoretically rendered the sitting room fireplace obsolete, no one has invented a better focus for a room than an open fire. Not only does it warm the room, it attracts people as irresistibly as moths to a candle. A real fire is also a fierce ever-changing source of light, reflected in every shiny surface. Just as the setting sun's rays may tint a frozen field a deceptively warm shade of orange, so firelight can transform a potentially harsh setting. The room pictured here is uncompromisingly modern in every respect except for the actual fire on the hearth. Without the firelight to cast a warm glow on walls and polished floor, the room could look uninviting and positively chilly – one effect of having excessive shiny surfaces in a room. Polished surfaces are best kept to a minimum if you are trying to achieve a cosy atmosphere. Firelight is a bright bold colour, a shade that looks best at evening, when it also casts the most dramatic shadows – especially if there is no other lighting.

This is my list of favourite haunts: places that I visit to be inspired and find special things. It cannot pretend to be a finite list; nevertheless it is a good start.

ALFIE'S ANTIQUE
MARKET
13–25 Church Street
London NW8 8DT
Tel: (020) 7723 6066 M/O
Huge covered antiques
market. Particularly good
for decorative antiques.

THE BLUE DOOR
74 Church Road
London SW13 0DQ
Tel: (020) 8748 9785
Old and new table linens,
checked and striped
cottons.

BRITISH FELT CO
14 Drakes Mews
Crownhill
Milton Keynes
Bucks
MK8 OER
Tel: (01908) 263304
M/O (minimum of £60)
Specializes in felt.

BROADWICK SILKS
9–11 Broadwick Street
London W1 VEN
Tel: (020) 7734 3320 M/O
Wonderful selection of
fabrics at good prices.

BRICK LANE MARKET
Brick Lane
Shoreditch
London E1
Sundays only, 8am–1pm.
A no-frills market. Plenty
of rubbish to wade
through, but always worth
it, as prices are realistic.

BRYONY THOMASSON
(by appointment only)
Tel: (020) 7731 3693
Antiques, wonderful
decorative and handwoven
textiles, rustic clothing
and objects.

CANDLE MAKERS'
SUPPLIERS
28 Blythe Road
London W14 0HA
Tel: (020) 7602 4031 M/O
Everything you need to
make candles and a huge
selection for sale.

CARDEN CUNIETTI
83 Westbourne Park Road
London W2 5QH
Tel: (020) 7229 8630 M/O
Exciting selection of
decorative objects as well
as pieces of furniture.

CATH KIDSTON
8 Clarendon Cross
London W11 4AP
Tel: (020) 7221 4000
M/O Tel: (020) 7229 8000
and
8 Elystan Street
London SW3
Household effects –
kitchen tables, dressers
and pretty cupboards with
the emphasis on fifties
style. Also fabrics,
blankets and quilts.

CELESTIAL BUTTONS
54 Cross Street
London N1 2BA

Tel/Fax: (020) 7226 4766
Beautiful shop offering a
huge selection of buttons
from around the world.

COLUMBIA ROAD
FLOWER MARKET
Columbia Road
London E2
Every Sunday morning
8am–2pm. Wide selection
of plants and cut flowers at
very cheap prices. Around
the market are shops
selling not only garden
related items but also bric-
a-brac, furniture and other
decorative things.

DECORATIVE LIVING
55 New King's Road
London SW6 4SE
Tel/Fax: (020) 7736 5623
Rustic and unique
furniture. Lots of
bric-a-brac.

DESIGNERS GUILD
267–277 Kings Road
London SW3 5EN
Tel: (020) 7351 5775
Richly coloured fabrics,
modern furniture and
other decorative items.

THE DORMY HOUSE
Stirling Park
East Portway Industrial
Estate, Andover
Hampshire SP10 3TZ
Tel: (01264) 365808 M/O
Supplies bedheads
suitable for covering.

*M/O: mail order
available*

EGG
36 Kinnerton Street
London SWIX 8ES
Tel: (020) 7235 9315
Simple accessories,
ceramics, textiles
and crafts.

FALKNER FINE PAPERS
76 Southampton Row
London WC1B 4AR
Tel: (020) 7831 1151 M/O
Exquisite papers from
around the world.

JUDY GREENWOOD
ANTIQUES
657 Fulham Road
London SW6 5PY
Tel: (020) 7736 6037
Antique patchwork quilts
and bedcovers, and beds.

IAN MANKIN
109 Regents Park Road
London NW1 8UR
Tel: (020) 7722 0997 M/O
Specializes in simple fabric
designs, especially checked
and striped tickings.

JOHN LEWIS
278–306 Oxford Street
London W1A 1EX
Tel: (020) 7629 7711 M/O
Full-scale department
store with excellent
haberdashery department.

KARA KARA
2A Pond Place
London SW3 6QJ
Tel: (020) 7591 0891

Beautiful wooden
furniture, objects and
fabrics from Asia.

LIBERTY
214 Regent Street
London W1R 6AH
Tel: (020) 7734 1234
Inspirational shop with
wonderful fabrics.

MINT
70 Wigmore Street
London W1H 9DL
Tel: (020) 7224 4406
Interesting pieces of
furniture, and other
decorative items.
Good on texture.

NICOLE FARHI HOME
17 Clifford Street
London W1X 1RG
Tel: (020) 7494 9051
Very expensive, but
always inspiring.

OSBORNE & LITTLE
304–308 Kings Road
London SW3 5UH
Tel: (020) 7352 1456
A good range of plain
linen fabrics in plenty
of colours.

OUT OF TIME
169B High Street
Street
Somerset BA16 OND
Tel: (01458) 448870
Rustic furniture and lots
of bric-a-brac, especially
thngs for the garden.

PORTOBELLO MARKET
London W10
Information (020) 7727 7684
A great atmosphere and
a variety of stalls selling
everything from antiques
and collectables to second-
hand clothes. I particularly
like the Portobello Green
market under the Westway
Bridge, on Fridays,
Saturdays and Sundays,
9am–4pm.

RAU
36 Islington Green
London N1 8DU
Tel: (020) 7359 5337
Richly coloured fabrics,
ceramics and other
decorative objects from
around the world.

ROWAN
Green Lane Mill
Holmfirth,
West Yorkshire HD7 1RW
Tel: (01484) 681881 for
stockists M/O
A huge selection of knitting
yarns in good colours.

RUSSELL & CHAPPLE
23 Monmouth Street
London WC2H 9DE
Tel: (020) 7836 7521 M/O
Suppliers of artist's
canvas and linens.

SUMMERILL & BISHOP
100 Portland Road
London W11 4LN
Tel (020) 7221 4566

Inspirational kitchenware,
cooking utensils and other
accessories.

TOBIAS AND THE ANGEL
68 White Hart Lane
London SW13 OPZ
Tel/Fax: (020) 8878 8902
Country-style kitchen
china and utensils, antique
linens and decorative pieces.

TOWN HOUSE
116 Columbia Road
London E2 7RG
Tel: (020) 7613 2866
Open Sunday mornings
10am–2pm or by
appointment.
Specializes in English
and French decorative
and painted antiques.

VV ROULEAUX
54 Sloane Square
London SW1W 8AX
Tel (020) 7730 3125
and
6 Marylebone High Street
London SW1H 3PB
Tel: (020) 7224 5179
Huge selection of ribbons,
cords and braids.

WHALEYS
Harris Court
Great Horton
Bradford
West Yorkshire BD7 4EQ
Tel: (01274) 576718 M/O
Calicos, cotton and
canvases in white,
natural and black.

Author's Acknowledgments

First, I wish to thank Pia Tryde for taking such beautiful pictures, and Georgina Rhodes for her consistent encouragement, vision and great art direction. I couldn't have asked for a better team nor one with such good humour. I would also like to say a big thank you to Jo Richardson, the editor, for all her support and dedication to the book. I am indebted to Melanie Sauze, for all her help with making up so many of the projects and to Bryony Thomasson, for supplying many of the wonderful fabrics. Always a joy to visit. I would like to say thank you to the following at Conran: Catriona Woodburn, Clare Limpus and particularly Leslie Harrington. Also to my agent, Fiona Lindsay and to Claudia Dulak for her assistance. On a personal front, a very special thank you to my husband Charles.

Conran Octopus would like to thank the following photographers and organizations for their kind permission to reproduce the photographs in this book: 2 Ingalill Snitt; 5 below left Jan Baldwin; 5 below right Adam Woolfitt/Robert Harding Picture Library; 6 left Mick Sharp; 6 right Mick Sharp/Jean Williamson; 7 left Ian Cumming/Axiom Photographic Agency; 7 right Jan Baldwin; 8 Ingalill Snitt; 9 Heather Angel; 10 left Jane Gifford; 10 right Luc Wauman; 11 left Andrew Wood/Homes & Gardens/Robert Harding Syndication; 11 right Steve Benbow/Impact; 12 Simon Whitmore/Homes & Gardens/Robert Harding Syndication; 13 above Marie Pierre Morel (stylist: Gerald Signe)/Marie Claire Maison; 13 below Andrew Wood/Homes & Gardens/Robert Harding Syndication; 18–19 David George/The World of Interiors; 20 Herbert Ypma/The Interior Archive; 20–21 Christian Sarramon; 30 right Jacqui Hurst; 31 Dick Scott-Stewart/The Special Photographers Library; 36 Ingalill Snitt; 38–39 John Perret/Tony Stone Images; 40 Ingalill Snitt; 42–43 Herbert Ypma/The Interior Archive; 43 Simon Upton (designer:Rupert Spira)/The Interior Archive; 48 Ingalill Snitt; 49 above left Ron Sutherland; 49 above right Vogue Entertaining; 49 below left Jan Baldwin; 50 Verne Fotografie; 51 Charles Coate/Impact; 52–53 Paul Ryan/International Interiors; 54 left Heather Angel; 55 left The National Trust Photographic Library; 55 right Ingalill Snitt; 56 Marijke Heuff; 57 Patricia Aithie/Ffotograff; 63 Jacqui Hurst; 70–71 Simon Upton (designer: Rupert Spira)/The World of interiors; 72–73 Jacqui Hurst; 73 Richard Packwood/Oxford Scientific Films; 76 left Nigel Cattlin/Holt Studio International; 76 right Carlos Navajas; 77 left David Cavagnaro; 77 right Andrew Lawson; 82 William Paton/Bruce Coleman; 83 above Andrew Lawson; 83 below Mick Sharp; 84 Simon Upton (artist: Celia Lyttleton)/The Interior Archive; 86–87 Mick Sharp/Jean Williamson; 94 left John Darling/Tony Stone Images; 94–95 Ingalill Snitt; 95 right Paul Ryan/International Interiors; 100 David Cavagnaro; 101 Marie Pierre Morel (stylist: Marie Kalt)/ Marie Claire Maison; 106 Andrew Lyttleton)/The Interior Archive; 107 left Andrew Lawson; 107 right Andrew Lawson (designer: Carol Klein, Glebe Cottage, Devon); 113 above K Sayer/Homes & Gardens/IPC Magazines 113 below Alexis Wallerstein/Impact; 114 Simon Upton (artist: Overwood/Celia); 115 Fritz von der Schulenburg/The Interior Archive; 116–117 Tim Beddow (architect: Arthur Duff)/The Interior Archive; 118–119 Alexandre Bailhache (stylists: M. Bayle & C. Puech)/ Marie Claire Maison; 121 Catriona Bass/Impact; 122 left Tim Clinch/The Interior Archive; 122 right Alex Ramsay (The Crooked House)/The World of Interiors; 126 left Jan Baldwin; 126 right Heather Angel; 127 Christian Sarramon; 134–135 Marie Pierre Morel (stylist: Daniel Rozenszroch)/Marie Claire Maison; 135 Christian Sarramon; 136 Marie Pierre Morel (stylist: C. Ardouin)/Marie Claire Maison; 137 David Cavagnaro; 138 Ingalill Snitt; 142 Jerry Harpur (Hatfield House).

All other photographs by Pia Tryde, specially commissioned by Conran Octopus.